The Ultimate

Jealousy Self Help Guide

How to Conquer Jealousy and Enjoy Trusting Relationships for Life

Jessica Minty

Table Of Contents

Introduction

I want to thank you and congratulate you for purchasing this book!

This book contains proven steps and strategies on how to identify jealousy problems and how to solve them. Maintaining a positive outlook and believing in oneself are two key solutions to the problems arising from jealousy (e.g. relationship gaps), and these two themes shall be explored all throughout the book.

Jealousy is an inevitable human emotion, but human emotions can always be controlled. This task may not be easy, but it is possible. Self-discipline, self-awareness and maturity are important factors in controlling one's emotions. If you feel that you are hopeless with your jealousy problems, then abandon those thoughts! You are not hopeless. This book will try to speak to you about your problem and will act as your guide and your "mentor" in the difficult task of conquering jealousy.

Thanks again for purchasing this book, I truly hope the best for you. Please take some time to stop by and LIKE our Facebook page:

https://www.facebook.com/joypublishing

With gratitude,

Jessica Minty

Chapter 1: Recognizing Jealousy

Understanding the nature of jealousy

Everybody gets jealous. It's a part of human nature. Jealousy is an inevitable human emotion that can be viewed from different aspects. When one gets jealous, two things are possible: first, one may feel inspired to do better and be better because he/she envies a desirable aspect visible in another person and he/she wants to embody that said desirable aspect; and second, one may take jealousy negatively and it may harm one's self-esteem, most especially if he/she sees a desirable aspect in another person yet he/she thinks that that desirable aspect is not and cannot be present within himself/herself. This latter possibility – jealousy being taken negatively – is a pressing emotional problem for human beings.

When taken negatively, jealousy tends to enable the mind to create make-believe scenarios, disrupt the normal cycle of human relationships, damage one's self-esteem and discontinue old habits. A common human relationship that can be disrupted by jealousy and is probably the one that is most damaged by jealousy, is a romantic relationship – may it be between husband and wife or simply boyfriend and girlfriend. Oftentimes, jealousy in its different manifestations is the cause of many splits, gaps or creases within a romantic relationship.

For this, it is important that the problem of jealousy is addressed within the person possessing the jealous feelings so that these damages can be prevented. On the other hand, it is important to be a master of one's own emotions because human relationships tend to be unpredictable – you must be preventive instead of reactive when it comes to these situations because relationships damaged by jealousy may or may not be reconciled, and this depends upon the person trying to overcome the problem.

Identify the problem within yourself

Jealousy has different ways of manifesting itself – it may be through a pressing feeling that something is wrong or has gone wrong, through paranoia, through developing distrust towards the other person, and the likes. While it is easy to say that one is feeling jealous with symptoms that vary from person to person, the greater challenge is identifying *what* triggered the jealous feelings and *how* did these appear.

When you think that you are feeling jealous towards something, it is important to specifically identify the problem by assessing yourself. You must know specifically what the problem is and how it emerged, and probably what can be done to fix the said problem. This self-assessment can be done by asking yourself the following questions:

- **What makes me jealous?** – This is probably the simplest question that you must ask yourself when it comes to addressing your problem of jealousy. However, even though it is a simple and common question, the answers are sometimes hard to come by. Sometimes, a person does not know what makes him/her jealous until the situation calls for it. This is why you must always be aware of yourself when it comes to these situations so that you can make mental notes on what to avoid in the future. This will also help you in preventing the same jealous feelings again.

- **Who is making me jealous?** – Aside from the basic task of identifying *what* exactly made you jealous, it is also important to identify *who* caused or triggered these feelings. It may be a person who lives an almost-perfect life, it may be your family member, or it may also be your romantic partner. In the context of a romantic relationship, this question may also be asked if there are certain people around your partner who you do not trust for some reason, thus making you feel jealous.

  In this case, it is important for you and your partner to talk about these people around him/her so that future problems arising from jealousy may be prevented. However, in general, identifying the person who has caused your jealousy is an important step so that you know who to talk to about your feelings – this does not only help you overcome your jealousy, but it also teaches the other person a lesson on a mistake that he/she must not do again. Most importantly, talking to the person who has caused your jealousy is a way of saving your relationship.

- **How do I get jealous?** – This question raises the issue of self-awareness. When a person is jealous, he/she tends to do or say things that he/she does not mean completely out of jealousy. This may cause misunderstandings among the people who have seen or heard your actions and words. To prevent this, it is important to always be aware of what you say and what you do. You can ask yourself the following questions: What do you do when you're jealous? What do you say? How do you act when things are just normal? How different do you act when you're jealous? You must know and master the answers to these questions so that you know for sure if you're feeling jealous or not, and so you can act on these situations immediately.

- **How do I stop being jealous?** – From identifying the things and the persons who make you jealous to how you act when you are jealous, the next step is to know how these negative emotions will fade away. Jealousy attracts negativity, thus it is not a safe option for you to let the feeling linger for too long. Answering this question may take a while, since there are different situations of jealousy and different ways of making these emotions subside, but as long as you are self-aware and you are willing to learn more about yourself and correct yourself, then you shouldn't have a problem in dealing with this question.

These questions may serve as your guide when dealing with jealousy, especially if you feel that it is already present. But underneath these guide questions lie another important challenge: the challenge of self-assessment.

The challenge of self-assessment

When you know that you are feeling jealous about something (given the different possible manifestations above and possibly other manifestations), you must be willing to assess yourself in order to find out how the jealousy incident happened. This way, things can be sorted out according to what issues are considered crucial and are in need of discussion. This takes a lot of self-discipline as well as acceptance because in the process, we might think that all our arguments are correct and our jealousy is fully justified, but you must also take into consideration what other people have to say.

Chapter 2: Trying to Overcome Jealousy

Once you have assessed yourself and you have already found out what and who make you jealous, then the next thing is to try to fix things and to prevent the problem from evolving into something bigger and more problematic. This can only happen if you are certain about what caused you to be jealous and if you know the exact persons to talk to about what you think and feel.

After patching things up with whomever you have had a rift with due to your jealousy, then you must strive not to let these incidents happen again. As mentioned before, human relationships are unpredictable. If arguments or misunderstandings due to jealousy can be fixed the first time, then there is no certainty that they can be fixed again in the future because the nature and the extent of one's jealousy varies on a case-to-case basis. This is why it is better if you learn how to overcome your jealousy instead of trying to see light in complete darkness when the drastic situation occurs again.

The following are some tips to overcome jealousy. Trying to do them once does not do the trick – you must always keep these tips in mind, especially when your jealousy gets constantly triggered. Just like the old saying, practice makes perfect. Practice these tips and surely you'll be able to overcome your jealousy.

- **Do not over think** – Over thinking and paranoia go hand-in-hand. They are both fatal triggers of the negative human emotions. If you engage yourself in over thinking and if you allow yourself to become paranoid in all situations, then you might end up constructing your own versions of reality and you might refuse to accept the *actual* reality that goes against your self-constructions. If you will your mind to construct these make-believe scenarios, then surely it will do so and it will be difficult for you to reverse what your mind has already constructed as the truth. Also, over thinking causes people to become more distrusting, meaning that you tend to doubt every single thing that a person explains to you.

This should not be the case. The key to overcoming paranoia is to be able to successfully separate make-believe from reality. If you know that something is not real, then there is no use in believing that it is; as this will only cause paranoia. A good option is to ask for other people's opinions on the matter in order to find out if something that you think is real or not.

People's opinions will differ, and it is up to you to weigh which opinion has more substance. A friendly reminder: as much as possible, remove the bias. Just because a person's opinion goes against your original thoughts does not mean that the person is not telling the truth. Be objective in judging other people's opinions and then make the big decision afterwards: to believe or not to believe.

- **Be more understanding** – Consider this situation: a man and a woman had a heated argument due to the woman being jealous upon seeing on Facebook the man's photo with another woman. The man then tries to explain that the woman in the photo is just a colleague and there should be nothing to worry about. If the woman allows paranoia to rule over her, then there is a possibility that she will not listen to the man's explanations and this will just result to further arguments and misunderstandings. Because of the woman's refusal to hear out the man's explanations and to think his words through, it damaged their relationship.

This situation only shows that every incident of jealousy must go with an explanation. First, you have to explain to yourself what caused the jealousy, who triggered it, and how it happened; second, the person/s who caused your jealousy must then explain himself/themselves to you in order to clear things out. The latter is crucial. If you refuse to let the second phase of explanations happen, then you are also refusing the possibility of mending your relationship.

Remember that when a person is jealous, he/she tends to hold on tightly to his/her own beliefs and does not immediately trust other people's opinions, except if these opinions agree with the already-existing assumptions. The question that arises here now is – what if your assumptions are wrong? What if you are just over thinking, or probably you are just feeling paranoid, thinking that the person who caused your jealousy is doing something wrong but he/she is not? The other perspectives of the story must also be considered in order to get a full view of things.

You must not settle with your own assumptions because you might end up wrong. This is why it is important to hear the other side of the story. And in hearing the other side of the story, bear in mind that you must listen with an open heart as well as open ears. Do not allow your negative and paranoid thoughts to overcome you.

Just listen to what the other person has to say because your assumptions might be wrong and may have only been caused by your paranoia. There is nothing wrong with mistaken assumptions – we all make mistakes, and this is a part of human nature. What is important is that when you are wrong, you know how to accept your mistakes and you also know that these are the things that you must not do in the future.

The bottom line here is that you must learn how to be understanding. You must lend your ears in order to hear out what other people have to say because if you do not, you might end up believing in something that is not true, and you might regret the fact that you wasted an opportunity to correct your mistaken assumptions. Other people's thoughts may or may not shed light on your doubts and questions, but to avoid suffering the negative consequences of jealousy, it does not hurt to listen.

- **Do not jump to conclusions** – An essential part of being more understanding towards other people is to avoid jumping to conclusions. When jealousy strikes, people are most likely to create scenarios with their respective endings in their own heads, and it is unlikely that they will listen to other people's explanations and corrections. It is important to be more understanding of the situation, but it is also important to let your constructed "conclusion" be falsifiable – meaning that you do not hold on to it as if it was the only real thing, rather, you allow for it to have alternative explanations and you are open to considering other possible conclusions. After all, your constructed conclusions may be wrong, and there is a possibility that the only way to prove them wrong and correct them is through listening to other people and considering their opinions.

- **Focus on your strengths and not your weaknesses** – In overcoming your paranoia, you must always believe in yourself. Focus on your strengths and not on your weaknesses. Thinking that you are weak will only make you feel bad, and this might trigger more negative thoughts. Insecurity is a top cause of jealousy, but bear in mind that there is no need to be insecure. Everyone has their own unique strengths and weaknesses – people will always compare, but you must know within yourself what you are and are not capable of. Do not be afraid to explore and unleash your inner strengths, and once you see them, do not deny them. They are precious gifts, and who knows? Other people may not have the same skills. Forget about your weaknesses and focus on believing in yourself. Remember that weaknesses may be turned into strengths, and strengths can be further improved. This is what you must strive for.

- **Uplift your self-esteem** – Lastly, in focusing on your strengths and highlighting your skills and talents as a person, you end up uplifting your self-esteem. In the process, you also learn what causes your self-esteem to diminish, and these causes are what you need to avoid in the future. In the end, you must keep that self-esteem high and never cease to believe in yourself. You will end up reducing a lot of insecurity-related jealousy incidents if you believe that there is nothing to be insecure about in other people. Happier and more stable relationships will then ensue. Check out my book, " Self Confidence Guide" to conquer your insecurity and achieve self esteem.

- **Be more trusting** – Trusting someone is not as easy as it sounds. When you give your trust to a person, you expect this person to keep it and not break it. It hurts when someone breaks your trust, but it doesn't mean that you have to stop trusting people. Jealousy causes people to be more distrusting – the paranoia and negative thoughts cause people to believe that no one can be trusted and that everybody is acting suspicious. This should not be the case.

If you keep on thinking that people cannot be trusted and if you refuse to trust people just because you have trust issues before, then it is unlikely that you will be able to solve your jealousy problems completely. Trust is an important component of overcoming jealousy. Even though you have experienced having your trust broken several times in the past, you must not stop trusting people. Even though they say that trust is earned and not given, it still helps to give people the chance to earn your trust.

When you become more trusting, it is unlikely that jealousy-induced incidents will occur as often as before. When you become more trusting, you doubt less and less and you also lessen the likelihood of creating your own scenarios and endings, thus successfully separating make-believe from reality. And when you become more trusting, you can stabilize your relationships with other people, may it be romantic or not, because there will be lesser conflicts due to trust issues. Basically, to become more trusting is a win-win situation for you: you overcome jealousy and you maintain happy and stable relationships.

The fact that overcoming jealousy is not easy must be acknowledged. It is difficult to battle with your own thoughts and emotions. On the other hand, the challenge of disciplining yourself is also not easy. There are times when you feel like you cannot stop over thinking and that paranoia is the best way to go because you believe that what you think is right but in the end, you must always remember not to let negativity embrace you completely.

Chapter 3: Comparison is a Frienemy

One way of overcoming paranoia is to focus on your strengths and not your weaknesses. Jealousy may occur if you feel inferior towards another person, thinking that this person is better than you and you are nothing compared to him. You must never have these thoughts – and if these thoughts happen to appear, do your best to dismiss them. Remember that everyone has their own special talents and skills to offer, and that no two people are exactly the same. You might feel that a person is better than you in everything, but maybe you are only saying that because you have not discovered your hidden talents yet. We all have our hidden talents waiting to be discovered at their own perfect time.

In my Self Confidence book, I talk about how we often compare our whole lives to the few minutes we see in another person's life. I have a friend in particular that is very impressive. For example, we were camping over the Easter weekend and she made a turkey! It can be easy for me to compare myself to her in that moment. I can quickly start feeling inadequate and jealous that she has it all together. However, I don't see the other parts of her life. I don't see what she sacrifices or who else suffers in order for her to do all that she does. I'm comparing apples to oranges when I do this.

Also, we must remember that we cannot please everybody. You may feel jealous about someone being the best at something, but do not forget that there is a possibility that you are meant for something else, and you just haven't found out yet. Do not lose hope in trying to look for your strengths – just stay focused on discovering them and they will unleash on their own. Once you succumb to negativity and you just settle for your weaknesses, your strengths may be too late to be discovered and improved.

How, then, are strengths and weaknesses related to jealousy? The answer is: comparison. Comparison is considered a "frienemy" – a friend and an enemy. Comparison works in two ways: it may lead towards a positive outlook and positive choices, or it may lead towards the negative.

- **Comparison as a friend**

  When comparison acts as a friend, the aspects that you compare with another person serve as your inspiration to do better. If you see that another person is good in sports for example and you do not even play sports, but you see that the person is also not athletic before but he/she only strived hard to be good in sports, then comparison at this point may be your inspiration to engage yourself in something that you have not tried before. Once you have found yourself thinking, *"I want to be just like that person"*, then you have found a friend in comparison. Therefore, your jealousy has been transformed into something better.

- **Comparison as an enemy**

  Comparison as an enemy is where the negative consequences of jealousy enter the picture. In this context, when you compare yourself with another person and you find out that the person has desirable characteristics that you do not have, then you end up being jealous, thinking that you are inferior to the person and you cannot be like him/her no matter how much you tried. This is the ugly part of comparison. But these kinds of thoughts only occur if your self-esteem is low. If you have high self-esteem, then you firmly believe in yourself and in your capabilities. This will ensure that there will be no negative thoughts that will continue to bother you.

People will not cease to compare. Human beings have the tendency to compare any two things that they see are not alike in order to shed light on their differences. These differences provide the distinction between the things, situations or objects being compared. In this context, your difference from another person probably in terms of attitude, personality, or character is what makes you unique. Just because you see something in another person that you do not see in yourself does not mean that you have to be disheartened. Like what was mentioned before, comparison works in two ways – it either inspires you or destroys you. Strive for the former. Make comparison your inspiration. As much as you want to be distinct from another person, there is no problem if another person possesses good qualities that you also want to acquire.

There is no need to be jealous because we are all capable of improving ourselves – it is only a matter of will and action. Try using your jealousy in a positive way. Instead of seeing it as negative and something that you must rid yourself of, see it as a tool. See jealousy as a clue that indicates there is something that you want that you don't yet have. Use it to catapult you towards the qualities or possessions you desire. There is no need to beat yourself up. Celebrate that you are feeling jealous and look for the message that it is sending you. Then start pursuing the necessary means for that to become a reality for your own life.

Keep in mind, this does not mean you take things from other people. I just want to make that clear. But if you're jealous because someone just bought a new car, use that jealousy as a sign that its important for you to a have a new car too. Use the jealousy to fuel you to achieve your goal. So often the emotion of jealousy can consume and drain us of our energy. Flip the coin and use it to empower you. I hope this is a new way of thinking for you.

Chapter 4: Maintain that Positive Outlook

Now that we have established the nature of jealousy, its different manifestations, tips on how to overcome it and the danger of comparison – we now move on to the most challenging part of it all: trying to maintain that positive outlook in life. Negativity lies at the core of jealousy. Negative thoughts trigger negative emotions. Like what they always say, consistency is the key. Be consistent in maintaining a positive outlook and you are assured that jealousy will bother you less and less.

A positive outlook is crucial especially in terms of insecurity. Just like what was mentioned in the previous chapters, you must focus on your strengths and not on your weaknesses and you must keep your self-esteem high. If you believe that you can, then you most definitely can. But if you believe that you are weak and that it is impossible for you to improve, then you will definitely have a hard time driving the negativity away in order to make room for the positive vibes. Maintaining a positive outlook will not only do you good, but it can also stabilize your relationships with other people for negative thoughts will be treated unwelcome, thus leaving all space for positivity to flourish.

How do you maintain a positive outlook? It is not an easy task, just as jealousy is an emotion that is not easy to conquer. It may be difficult, but it is possible. Here are some general tips on how to maintain a positive outlook in life:

- **Improve your outlook; shift from negative to positive.** – It's simple. How can you maintain a positive outlook if you do not even have a positive outlook to begin with? Also, improving your outlook is an essential step in improving yourself in general. If you refuse to believe that you are capable of doing something, then chances are you will lose all motivation to get rid of jealousy as well as other negative feelings and thoughts. On the other hand, being positive and believing that you *can* improve and you can conquer jealousy will produce positive results.

- **Continue to improve yourself** – In the preceding chapters, tips on how to overcome jealousy have been presented. Aside from being tips on overcoming jealousy, these are also tips on improving oneself. Improvement is a continuous process, and it starts with identifying the problem within yourself and goes on to taking concrete steps to address this problem.

  However, it does not stop with addressing the problem – you now have to strive hard for your efforts not to go to waste. Make sure that previous mistakes will not be committed again; especially if you know that these previous mistakes had cost you a lot. You will make new mistakes in the process of striving to improve yourself further, but what is important is that you utilize the life lessons that you have acquired in the past in order to correct these mistakes.

- **Think of the positive consequences of overcoming jealousy** – We all need some motivation for us to achieve a very challenging task. In this case, one of the possible motivations a person may have can be the positive consequences that may result from overcoming jealousy. The most common consequence will be having stable relationships with your peers – free from doubts and misunderstandings with other people. Subsequent positive consequences arise from other consequences. Following these stable relationships is the consequence of living a peaceful life due to the absence of jealousy and envy. Aside from these, there are many other positive consequences of the absence of jealousy.

With these thoughts in mind, you might be more motivated to pursue your task and achieve it. It might take a long time and if you feel like giving up, just remember these motivations and these positive consequences for your much-needed boost of determination. After all, undergoing the difficult process of conquering jealousy is worth it if you can see that it has positive results in the end.

- **Maintain a support group** – A support group does wonders. There's nothing wrong with trying to improve yourself on your own, but it also helps to have other people who will guide you in your journey to conquering jealousy and other negative feelings. These people will motivate you in times of doubt, and they will be the ones to remind you how much you have achieved. A support group usually consists of your most-trusted friends or relatives, or it may also consist of people who are going through the same experiences.

Usually, people with the same experiences supporting each other are preferred because they do not only motivate others not to give up, but they are also helping themselves get motivated by allowing themselves to be surrounded by people who understand what they are going through. Having people who understand you completely is an essential part of improving yourself because it helps you to realize that not everyone will judge you for your actions, instead there are still people who believe in you and your capabilities.

A support group also serves as your outlet for your feelings. There are a lot of possible outlets such as your hobbies, a journal, a blog, and the likes; but talking to people who know what you are going through is the best outlet. Do not keep your feelings to yourself because this will just cause you to over think. Tell other people what you feel, and listen to their pieces of advice. Who knows? They probably know what is best for you. Do not be afraid to ask other people for advice – rather, it is the right thing to do.

In being part of a support group, you must also do your duties as a member of the said group. As much as other people are helping you in your journey to conquer jealousy and the other negative human emotions, you must also do your part in doing the same. Besides, all hard work pays off. Once you see that you have helped someone conquer his/her jealousy issues, then it will give you a sense of self-fulfillment.

If you are feeling hopeless or if you feel that you can never win over jealousy, do not be disheartened. Believe in yourself and think of the great possibilities and good opportunities that come with conquering jealousy. Keep in mind that jealousy does not do you any good, thus it does not deserve to stay in your life. Maintain that positive outlook and eventually, you'll say goodbye to jealousy problems.

It is not easy to conquer jealousy. We cannot always control these negative emotions, but we can always control how we react to the situations that we face and how we face our problems. In this, maturity is the key. One must be mature enough to differentiate what is right from wrong, and be humble enough to accept his/her own mistakes and strive to improve himself/herself. Aside from maturity, determination is also important. In striving to conquer jealousy and maintain healthy and trusting relationships, one must be determined to reach the goal. Since this is not an easy task, giving up is a quick available option. You must not consider this option – just think of all the happy possibilities that will follow after achieving your goal. Keep those in mind, and you'll eventually succeed.

The journey is never an easy one. Nothing good comes without hard work. Conquering jealousy does not come in the blink of an eye, but through hard work, patience, and self-discipline, it is possible.

Conclusion

Thank you again for purchasing my book.

I hope this book was able to help you recognize the nature of jealousy, overcome your jealousy problems, and maintain a positive outlook in order to prevent negativity from taking over your emotions and to maintain healthy relationships with your peers.

The next step is to absorb and internalize the tips and strategies provided in this book and to apply them in real life. As extensive as you might be in reading about conquering your jealousy problems, the real challenge remains: applying these theories and tips in real life. Only then can you see the effects of your actions and you will be able to assess if the tips are effective for you or not. In doing so, you are doing yourself a favor of not committing future mistakes on the same matter.

I really encourage you to see your jealousy in a positive light. Search for the reason why you are feeling jealous and what causes you to feel threatened. If you are jealous because some thing is lacking in your life or there is a personal attribute you are attracted to, then use your jealousy to propel you in that direction.

In addition, please remember to check out our Facebook page in order to find other resources and upcoming promotions:

https://www.facebook.com/joypublishing

With sincere thanks, Jessica Minty

Preview Of "Codependency Guide: How to Be Codependent No More and Have Healthy Relationships for Life"

Chapter 1 – What is Codependency?

Most people are not aware that codependence is an addiction. In fact, it is the most common of all the types of addictions; it is the addiction of looking elsewhere to find happiness and fulfillment. Instead of finding it inside yourself, you try to find your happiness in people and in things that you might lose, like places, experiences, behaviors, things and relationships.

Essentially, your life is defined by that relationship. You are addicted to that relationship. Your behavior, thoughts, and emotions become intertwined with another in an unbalanced manner. You lessen yourself and place the relationship on a pedestal above you. You will do whatever it takes to keep that relationship happy and healthy. Codependency deceives you into thinking that you can control your interior feelings by controlling exterior sources in the form of people, feelings or things. At the core of codependency is control or the lack of control in a person's life.

Unknowingly, people who are codependent put a label on themselves, and labels will never empower you. Labels have become acceptable in today's society as codependency becomes almost synonymous with romance and relationships. However, codependency can often be confused with sacrificial love or martyrdom. But isn't that what love is all about? Giving yourself completely and wholly towards another? Unfortunately, people who are in codependent relationships may not be aware that they are in relationships characterized as such. It is both hard to recognize and hard to end.

Codependent Patterns

It is important to recognize the patterns characteristic of a codependent person. These attributes may snap you out of denial if you didn't think you had codependent tendencies up until this point. Or you'll realize your areas of weakness where attention needs to be given.

As a codependent, you:
- Assume responsibility for others' feelings and behaviors
- Feel guilty about other's feelings and behaviors
- Have difficulty identifying what you are feeling or difficulty expressing feelings
- Are afraid of your own anger, yet sometimes erupt in rage
- Worry about how others may respond to your feelings, opinions, and behavior
- Have difficulty making decisions
- Are afraid of being hurt and/or rejected by others
- Minimize, alter or deny how you truly feel
- Are very sensitive to how others are feeling and feel the same
- Are afraid to express differing opinions or feelings
- Value others opinions and feelings more than your own
- Embarrassed to receive recognition and praise, or gifts

- Judge everything you think, say, or do harshly, as never "good enough"
- Are a perfectionist
- Are extremely loyal, remaining in harmful situations too long
- Do not ask others to meet your needs or desires
- Do not perceive yourself as lovable and worthwhile
- Compromise your own values and integrity to avoid rejection or others' anger

(Taken from a Celebrate Recovery resource: "Codependency – The Problem and Solution for Women")

Do you recognize some of these patterns in yourself? You may have one or many. You may be relieved or overwhelmed. Take heart, you are not alone. Keep in mind that people fall on a continuum. Some people can have codependent tendencies that only surface in a particular circumstance. Others are engrossed in codependency and can't even leave the house to put gas in their car. While there are always extremes, a majority of the population falls in the middle. Everybody, to some extent, and at some point in their life, will exhibit codependent tendencies in some form or another.

Hopefully, you have been able to identify your own codependent patterns that you can start bringing healing to. It is not until the darkness has been brought to the light does the healing begin. Knowledge of where you stand with codependency is powerful. You have a clear picture of the enemy you are trying to slay. You have clarity and a target to set your focus upon. You are that much closer to victory...

Check out the rest of this book on Amazon

Or go to: http://amzn.to/1bPS76Z

Check Out My Other Books

Below you'll find some of my other books also available on Amazon and Kindle. Search for these titles on the Amazon website to find them.

Anxiety Relief: Anxiety Management & Stress Solutions for Overcoming Anxiety, Worry & Dread to Emotional Health, Anxiety Free & Stress Relief

Codependency: A Relationship Rescue for Toxic Relationships, Manipulation & Enabling to Self Confidence, Boundaries, Emotional Health & Happiness ****BEST SELLER***

EFT Tapping: Emotional Freedom to Break Free From Cravings, Temptation & Bad Habits to Emotional Health, Stress Relief & Happiness

Jealousy: A Relationship Rescue for Overcoming Fear, Insecurity, Trust Issues, Lying & Envy to Trust & Healthy Relationships

Manipulation: A Relationship Rescue for Breaking Free from Bad Relationships, Mind Control, Emotional Abuse & Codependency to Reclaiming Your Self Confidence & Sanity

Mindfulness Meditation: Mindfulness & Anxiety Management for Overcoming Anxiety & Worry to Emotional Health, Inner Peace & Happiness

Perfectionism: Letting Go of Mistakes & Overcoming Anxiety, Perfection & Procrastination to Victory & Self Acceptance

Self Confidence: Breaking Free from Shyness, Insecurity & Shame to Self Care, Self Acceptance & Self Esteem

Willpower: Breaking Free From Cravings, Temptation & Bad Habits to Self Control, Self Discipline & Goal Setting

One Last Thing...

thank you soooooooooo much

If you believe that this book is worth sharing, would you please take the time to let others know how it affected your life? If it turns out to make a difference in the lives of others, they will be forever grateful to you, as will I.

Printed in Great Britain
by Amazon